Another Bloody Mountain:

Prisoner of War and Escape in Italy 1943

Vic Duke

Iron City Publications

Published in 2011 by Iron City Publications

www.ironcitypublications.com

ironcity@btinternet.com

ISBN 978-0-9559212-1-6

Printed by Print Bureau, Hebden Bridge (tel: 01422-847799)

INTRODUCTION

My father, Wallace Douglas (Wally) Duke, was a regular soldier serving with the Kings Own Royal Regiment in India, when the Second World War broke out. He first saw action in Iraq in 1941, and was then sent to North Africa in 1942 as part of the 10th Indian Division. Captured during the first battle of El Alamein in June 1942 (which Rommel won), he was taken to Italy as a prisoner of war. Following the Italian Armistice, he escaped from camp PG53 at Sforzacosta on 15th September 1943, and commenced a 30 day walk through the Apennine mountains to reach the advancing British front line.

This book is my account of his capture, life as a POW, and subsequent escape route. It is based on a combination of fact, fiction and fieldwork. My father often recited tales of this period, which I can recall by heart. Echoing the experience of many sons, my lingering questions remained unasked until it was too late. My father died in 2002. Now finally, through extensive research in the UK and intensive fieldwork in Italy, allied to my father's own tales, I can reveal a reasonably accurate portrayal of his story.

Word of mouth eye witness accounts provide factual evidence of a certain kind. My father's tales were repeated many times over several decades, always virtually identical in detail, which affords a high degree of authenticity. Sometimes, orally obtained 'facts' can be misleading. My father always said that he was in a prison camp in Ancona. I assumed that this meant the city of Ancona on the Adriatic coast, and searched for evidence of a camp in the city. Only after considerable research did I discover that his camp, PG53, was actually located in the village of Sforzacosta, which is in the province of Ancona, some 50 km south west of the city.

On the other hand, individual accounts can provide a clue to a location, which can then be tracked down by diligent research. One of my father's tales concerned his crossing of the Gran Sasso mountain range with the help of two Italian partisans. They pointed out to him an *albergo* (inn), where Benito Mussolini was held captive by the partisans only weeks before. I was able to identify the inn as La Villetta in Fonte Cerreto, which helped me to plot my father's course across the Gran Sasso, and moreover, link this to the probable trails before and after the Gran Sasso.

Interestingly, I found out from my Aunt Dorothy, my father's sister, that my father began writing his own version of the Italian adventure, shortly after repatriation to the UK. However, later, during a bout of bad temper, to which he was prone after the war, my father burnt the entire draft, on the grounds that nobody would be interested.

More objective factual background was acquired from general histories of the Kings Own regiment, the North African campaign, and POWs in Italy. A bibliography is provided at the end of the book. Also consulted were seven book length accounts by individual escapees in Italy, some of whom were imprisoned in PG53. A common theme in all the personal accounts is the tremendous hospitality and courage of the local peasantry (*contadini*) in the Marche and Abruzzo regions. Details of my father's army service were obtained from the Army Personnel Centre in Glasgow, which confirmed some key dates. I also found a news report in the Lincolnshire Times of 18th December 1943, describing his escape and return to the UK. A copy of this, along with my father's photo, follows this introduction. In response to the newspaper article, which gave his address, my father received many letters from desperate wives, mothers or girlfriends seeking any news of their loved ones. Thirteen of these letters survived in his possessions, and make sad reading. Not recognising any names, my father didn't reply to any of them.

Official escape reports are lodged in the War Office records in the National Archives at Kew. Unusually, my father has two escape reports in the War Office records (I found only one other person with two). The first (in WO208/5395) was conducted in October 1943, shortly after reaching the British lines; and the second (in WO208/3319) dated as March 1944. A strange discrepancy between the two reports concerns the number in my father's original escape party – five in the first account and six in the second. My recollection is of my father always mentioning a group of five, which soon split into a three and a two.

As well as my father's escape reports, I also examined 124 other War Office reports of POWs who had escaped from PG53. These provided detailed yet contradictory evidence of the days following the Italian armistice, leading up to the mass escape on 15th September. Including my father's two reports, 108 are listed in the section entitled 'POWs in Italy who travelled south', and 18 are listed in the general Escape and Evasion reports.

As for the few fictional aspects of my account, these relate to some incidents along the escape route, of which I know what happened, but don't know exactly where. It makes for a better narrative to locate these incidents in a particular place, rather than somewhere round about here. For instance, I don't know for sure where my father exchanged clothing with an Italian peasant. I do know roughly how far along the route it was.

The fieldwork element refers to an eight day trip to Italy in September/October 2009, in order to visit the site of camp PG53, and then attempt to follow my father's escape route (by car). My trip was timed to coincide with the middle period of my father's 30 day walk, so as to replicate, as near as possible, the weather conditions he will have experienced.

A combination of his official escape report and my father's tales yielded the basic framework of the escape route. In addition, I found three old photos in my father's possessions, which were taken during his service in India. However, on the back were written Italian names, which proved to be lists of villages, all in a row, and they clearly formed part of his journey. My being in the field helped to resolve some uncertainties. Many an old track/path, linking two places on his route, was discovered easily, either visibly or by consulting locals. By the end of the trip I was confident of around 90% of my father's itinerary.

I was unprepared for the splendid scenery and beautiful autumn colours in the Apennines. My father never mentioned anything about the grandeur of the landscape he travelled through, his mind was focussed entirely on security and survival. The book contains many photos along the route, and thus serves as a travelogue for the Marche and Abruzzo. As a result I decided to publish the book with colour photos, even though this option was more expensive. All the photos in the text were taken by the author.

Thanks are due to my daughter, Rosie, and her partner Paul, for creating the front cover. The camp barbed wire photo on the back cover was provided by Andrea Manenti. Indeed I am greatly indebted to my eldest daughter's Italian partner, signore Andrea Manenti. He accompanied me on the trek through the Apennines in 2009, acting as my chauffeur and interpreter, as well as exuding good companionship. At the site of camp PG53, a local expert, Roberto Cruciani, was most helpful. Welcome overnight accommodation in Italy was freely supplied by Anna Sestili, Cristina Cleri and Valentina Varano. I am doubly beholden to Cristina, who also deciphered the writing on the back of one of the Indian photos, pointing out that it referred to a village and three named individuals. Giuseppe Millozzi kindly let me have an English language version of his Ph.D thesis on Allied POWs in the Marche, which formed the basis of his Italian book. The late Roger Absalom pointed me in the direction of the War Office escape reports, and advised me to contact the Monte San Martino Trust in London. The trust is a charity, which allocates scholarships for study in England to young Italians, in recognition of the help given to British escapees on the run. A portion of the proceeds from the sale of this book will be donated to the Trust. Everyone at The Monte San Martino Trust was most helpful, especially the secretary, the dedicated and charming Letitia Blake. Mention should also be made of Steve Sims, who gave me the exact reference to one of my father's escape reports, the very day before I was going to the National Archives at Kew.

Useful advice and information was received from Peter Donnelly, the curator of the Kings Own Regimental Museum in Lancaster. The staff at the National Archives were invariably helpful. During research visits to the archives, accommodation was willingly furnished by Roy and Margaret Satterthwaite in East Finchley. The librarians at my local library in Hebden Bridge assisted greatly in ordering or sending for books relevant to my task. Finally, thanks to my two daughters, Maddy and Rosie, for reading early drafts of the book.

Escaped P.O.W. Home

A Scunthorpe prisoner of war in Italy, who left his prison camp 53 near Ancona when the country fell, reaching the British lines over 200 miles away in 30 days, has arrived home.

He is L.-Cpl. Wallace D. Duke, aged 28, son of Mrs Griffin, of 40, King Edward-st., Scunthorpe, and the late Mr Duke.

L.-Cpl. Duke was captured near El Alamein in Libya in June, 1942, and describes his treatment in Italian prison camps as "rather poor," particularly during the first few month. Red Cross parcels, coming through within a short time, helped the men tremendously.

His 40 days' leave will extend over Christmas and the New Year, and he is hoping to meet all old friends again for the first time for well over a couple of years.

L.-Cpl. Duke and his parents lived in Hull for 17 years, and for two years before that time were at the Red Lion Hotel, Brigg.

WALLACE DOUGLAS DUKE

INDIA circa 1938

LINCOLNSHIRE TIMES

18 December 1943

ANOTHER BLOODY MOUNTAIN: PRISONER OF WAR AND ESCAPE IN ITALY 1943

1. <u>Capture in North Africa</u>

There is a conundrum re the exact date of Wally's capture. Official recognition as a POW is listed as 30th June 1942 at El Daba in Egypt. However, his army records also show that he was declared missing on 28th June, which means that Wally did not return to his unit at the end of that day. A transit camp for POWs was set up at El Daba around the 30th June, as the Allied forces retreated to El Alamein. My interpretation of this conundrum is that he was captured and picked up by the Germans on the 28th, and handed over to the Italians at the newly established El Daba camp on the 30th.

In terms of the wider context, his capture was a consequence of the rapid German advance eastwards following the fall of Tobruk on 21st June. On the 24th the 1st Batallion Kings Own took up a defensive position west of Mersa Matruh (in Egypt) at a crossroads, known as Charing Cross, which formed the junction between the Siwa and Sidi Barrani roads. The battalion was extended over a wide area with section posts 600 yards apart and a series of pathways linked these posts with HQ. On the 27th enemy tanks threatened to break through on the left, shelling intensified, communications with HQ were disrupted, and considerable confusion ensued. Indeed brigade HQ was moved back at 7pm. By the next morning the German Panzers had cut the road to the east of Mersa Matruh, meaning that direct retreat east was not possible.

On the morning of the 28th, Wally was in charge of a truck distributing supplies, including ammunition. As a regular soldier, Wally sensed that there was something wrong. There were no lookouts on the ridges and a general lack of an Allied presence. Suddenly a group of vehicles including armoured cars came over the ridge and approached the truck – they were German. As the senior soldier in the truck, Lance Corporal Duke immediately ordered the others not to resist. Given the ammunition in the rear, any resistance would have been fatal. Wally often recalled his conversation with the German Officer, who spoke excellent English.

'For you the war is over'.

'Maybe'.

'We are going to Cairo'.

'I don't think so'.

Wally and the others were put in a German truck along with an armed guard. Whilst on the move they were shelled by the British artillery and also strafed by RAF planes, which caused them to take cover by the side of the track. Their first destination was a prisoner collection point, which comprised a large circle of stones in the desert.

2. With the Germans

Wally always spoke highly of his treatment by the German soldiers, they were very correct and polite. In addition to the standard ration of dark bread and weak coffee, some of the Germans shared their food and drink with the captives. Wally managed to hold on to his personal possessions (including the Indian army photos later used in Italy to write the names of Italian villages on the back), something which did not occur for those captured by the Italians. Compared with other theatres of war, the North African campaigns were noted for the restraint and chivalry displayed by both sides.

The next day (the 29th) whilst still in German hands, there was an enthusiastic commotion in the camp. Soldiers excitedly shouted 'Rommel kommt', and Wally witnessed the great pride and respect shown by the German soldiers for their military commander. (Wally also reported an incident earlier in June when German planes bombed a Red Cross tent. The next day a German plane dropped leaflets signed by Rommel stating that those involved would be punished).

An agreement existed between the Axis powers in North Africa that all Allied POWs would be handed over to the Italians once secured behind the front line. As a result Wally was handed over to the Italian army at the POW transit camp in El Daba. The German officer apologised for this which puzzled Wally. 'You will see' he said.

3. With the Italians

Wally soon realised what the German officer meant. Initially the Italians in their green uniforms were universally loathed by Allied POWs. Living conditions were much worse, sanitary arrangements were poor or nonexistent, meals were insufficient and tasteless, and most seriously, disease was rife. In addition most of the Italian soldiers did not show the prisoners the respect afforded them by the Germans. Some of Mussolini's Alpine troops, with large feathers in their hats, laughed and jeered at the POWs.

After a couple of days Wally was herded along with other POWs onto trucks, where they were packed like sardines, for the journey westward. Probably there was an overnight stop at the POW transit camp at Derna, before proceeding to the Italians' main POW camp in Benghazi. Here there was a long wait for transportation by ship to the Italian mainland.

The journey along the North African coast was not all barren desert but in fact scenic in places, at least for those both fit enough and in a position to see out. From El Daba the trucks headed through Hafaya Pass and down into Sollum, where the bay glowed in shades of aquamarine, turquoise and silver. Sollum was the last settlement in Egypt before crossing into Libya. Along the Libyan coast the trucks passed by the Gazala cliffs and through the pretty seaside village of Derna, with its gardens, vines, figs, pomegranates and bananas. Finally, down onto the open plain approaching Benghazi, where the salt flats were blinding in the afternoon sun.

4. Benghazi POW camp

Incarceration at Benghazi was a terrible experience. The camp was huge yet still grossly overcrowded. Toilet facilities consisted of a large open hole in the ground, which was invariably covered in flies. The combined effects of the hot sun in the day, the bitter cold at night, overcrowded tents, limited food and water supplies, inadequate washing and toilet facilities, swarms of flies and mosquitoes, infestations of lice and fleas, all together made life almost unbearable. Not surprisingly disease was rampant, especially dysentery. No wonder the British POWs sarcastically christened their temporary home 'The Palms'.

Benghazi camp was situated in a valley and completely surrounded by four rows of barbed wire fencing, stranded and rolled. Elevated sentries were placed at 30 yard intervals outside the wire, and machine guns were stationed in each corner. Sentries were under strict orders to shoot any POW who touched the trip-wire, which was located a few feet inside the fence at knee height.

All the POWs were housed in Italian canvas tents, which were made up of groundsheets buttoned together over an oblong frame. Inside the tent they slept on the bare ground. Eventually blankets were issued to the POWs. Prisoners had to get up at dawn for the morning roll call, which often took an hour to complete. Breakfast consisted of a weak coffee made from acorns. At 11am POWs were issued with a bread bun, occasionally accompanied by a small piece of cheese. In the evening a hot liquid meal was served, which consisted predominantly of water.

It was at Benghazi that Wally developed dysentery. Many died from dysentery in the camp, but Wally survived through a combination of prior knowledge and sheer willpower. During his period as a medical orderly in Bangalore Hospital, he learned that if you have dysentery, it is fatal to eat any food. Accordingly he resisted the pangs of hunger for several days and gave away his bread and evening bowl of food to comrades in the tent. Initially they refused to take it, but he told them 'if you won't have it, I'll give it to someone else'. Amazingly Wally survived but in a very weak condition, little more than a living skeleton.

5. By ship to Italy

Around the beginning of August, Wally's name came up for transportation to Italy. The POWs were made to walk from the camp to the port, passing through the town where some Italian colonists hurled insults and stones at them. Just before dusk several hundred prisoners went slowly up the gangplank in single file onto an Italian merchant ship. Conditions on the ship were abominable. Around 500 men were crammed into the hold, after which the hatch was battened down, leaving the men in complete darkness, a veritable hell on earth. It was so crowded that prisoners couldn't move without touching a fellow unfortunate. Not to mention the rats scurrying around in the hold.

Two large latrine buckets were placed in the centre of the hold. Anyone desperate enough to want to use them had to clamber over the bodies of comrades in the dark. In the morning (the journey to the

Italian mainland took 2 days) the buckets were hoisted up by ropes on to the deck, depositing some of their load on the way up. Once on deck the buckets were emptied and hosed out. On each of the two mornings the POWs were allowed on deck in small groups to get drinking water from a tap. For the prisoners the whole of the two day journey was fraught with fear. Italian merchant ships were legitimate targets for Allied planes and submarines. At any time the vessel could have been sunk, laying in the dark was akin to being buried alive. On arrival at the port of Brindisi on the Adriatic east coast of Italy, the POWs were hosed down on deck before disembarking. Blinking in the sunlight, they could see the two little bays either side of Brindisi harbour.

6. Transit camps in Italy

The Italian authorities were not prepared for the large influx of Allied POWs from North Africa, so most of the prisoners spent varying amounts of time in a series of transit camps, whilst awaiting the preparation and completion of the permanent POW camps. Wally spent the first ten days in Italy at PG85 Tuturano near Brindisi, before moving to PG87 at Benevento, where he stayed until the beginning of November 1942. I know little of this period. His last transit camp was PG66 at Capua for ten days in November.

From Brindisi harbour the POWs were marched to the railway station for onward travel to Tuturano 10 km to the south, and the Italian authorities did not waste the opportunity to indulge in a spot of Fascist propaganda. Loudspeakers in the town boasted of Italian victory and Allied defeat, the starving POWs in poor condition looked suitably dejected, and the Italian civilian onlookers hissed and jeered. At the rail station the prisoners were loaded onto cattle trucks, 40 to a truck. However, this compared favourably with conditions on the ship.

Later there were two more journeys in cattle trucks to other transit camps, first to Benevento in August and then on to Capua in November. After arriving at Capua station the POWs faced a 15 minute walk to the camp. The route did not involve going through the town, its ancient monasteries were visible a mile away. Children looked down in wonder at the bedraggled prisoners from a school window and the route also passed a row of three-storey houses. Once ensconced at Capua PG66 an interesting feature to relieve the boredom was the visibility of Mount Vesuvius with smoke and flames rising in the distance.

Capua camp's layout was similar to that described previously at Benghazi. Barbed wire fencing surrounded the camp, and in each corner stood a sentry box containing a machine gun and a searchlight. At night a visit to and from the toilets was accompanied by one's own personal spotlight. Every POW received two blankets and the tents each housed fifteen men. One distinct improvement at Capua was a decent wash-house with plentiful water. The everyday routine at Capua was also similar to Benghazi. Roll call at dawn was followed by acorn coffee for breakfast. At lunchtime prisoners received a bowl of soup or skilly, which is a kind of thin gruel.

After little over a week at Capua, Wally learned that he was to be transferred to a permanent POW camp. Before removal to a permanent camp POWs were subjected to a ritual delousing. They stripped off their clothes, which were cleansed in industrial dry-cleaning machines. Then each prisoner had all his hair shaved off, which would take nine months to grow back fully. The final preparation for moving involved an official registration process. A photo and fingerprints were taken, and each prisoner's next of kin and home address was recorded.

7. Arrival at PG53 Sforzacosta

Towards the end of November, Wally was given a bread roll and a Red Cross parcel, and then set off with a large group of prisoners to Capua station. Another long journey in a cattle truck beckoned. En route Wally's train passed through Rome, but the POWs could see little from the cattle trucks. Wally was fond of saying that he had been to Rome but not seen it. The train then traversed the main spine of Italy, and snow capped mountains were clearly visible. At Fabiano the train turned off the main line, onto the Porto Civitanova branch line.

Along a stretch of single track, the train slowly ground to a halt at the destination station. For those who bothered to look, the station sign indicated Urbisaglia-Sforzacosta. Urbisaglia was a large hill town 6 km away, and Sforzacosta the small village in which both the station and camp PG53 were located.

The station itself was an imposing two storey building (see figure 1). It was located just off the main road, about 200 metres down a side street.

figure 1 Urbisaglia-Sforzacosta station

The prisoners were marched along the one main street in Sforzacosta, which at the time was part of the main road between Macerata and Tolentino. At the main junction in the village the P78 road heads south towards Ascoli.

On the left at the junction, the formidable outer wall of the camp emerged into view (see figure 2). In 1942 the wall was not as overgrown as now.

figure 2 the outer wall of camp PG53

The prisoners turned left at the junction and marched the last 200 metres to the main gate. With the gate opened, entry was through a sturdy arch, several metres thick (see figure 3).

figure 3 the main gate and arched entrance

PG53 was a POW camp for other ranks, not officers, and was located in an old factory. Administratively the camp was divided into three sectors, each comprising a large rectangular building, and each regarded as capable of accommodating 2,000 prisoners.

Immediately to the left after entering the gate was the guard room, manned in figure 4 by a particularly nasty looking Italian guard.

figure 4 the guard room

Around 100 metres past the guard room, the POWs turned left and ahead of them on the right were the gaunt grey factory buildings (see figure 5). The nearest block of buildings constituted sector 2, and the farthest in the distance formed sector 3, which was to be Wally's home for the next nine months.

figure 5 nearest is sector 2 and in the distance sector 3

8. Life at PG53

Although allocated to a sector for the purposes of administration and sleeping arrangements, the prisoners were allowed to walk freely between the sectors during daylight hours. The kitchens comprised two low rise one-storey buildings at the far end of sectors 2 and 3, away from the road. Beyond the kitchens was a large recreational field, which was open to everyone, either for individual exercise or for collective sporting contests such as football and cricket matches. Barbed wire was employed around the sports field and also on top of the camp wall. Along the perimeter were to be found the usual wooden towers, manned by sentries with machine guns and searchlights.

Sector 3 was a long rectangular building (figure 6), topped by two sections of barrel roofing (visible in figure 5). The large rooms, each accommodating around 750 men, had high ceilings with only a couple of windows located high up close to the roof. Wooden bunk beds were stacked three tiers high and adorned with straw mattresses.

figure 6 the long side of sector 3

On the outer edge of the recreational area, a trip wire ran the length of the fence, placed a few metres inside the fence at about knee height. Stepping beyond the trip wire was prohibited, and it was stated that anyone doing so was liable to be shot. Wally often spoke of an incident at the camp where a prisoner was shot by a trigger happy Italian sentry. All the POWs were furious and the sentry had to be removed from his post in order to forestall a riot. This incident occurred on 24th February 1943, as confirmed by a fellow POW's written account. A prisoner named Aaron, who had just arrived at PG53 the day before, was shot whilst urinating a couple of metres inside the trip wire.

Routine was paramount at PG53, each day resembling every other day. Reveille was at 6am. All that was provided for breakfast was a drink of acorn coffee, most men using an empty tin as a cup. The first of two daily roll calls occurred at 7.30am, taking place in the recreational field in all weathers. With up to 7,500 lined up in the field, roll call often took a couple of hours or more. The prisoners shivered in the cold, sweltered in the heat, and got soaked in the rain. It was common for several men to faint during roll call.

At around 10am the daily bread ration was distributed, which consisted of a small roll, occasionally augmented by a small piece of cheese. This formed one of the day's highlights. The day's second roll call took place at 3pm, again in all weathers. Late afternoon brought the only hot meal of the day, a bowl of the aforementioned skilly or watery soup, which contained negligible portions of macaroni and vegetables, and very rarely tiny bits of meat. Old hands who had spent months at the camp, carefully judged their location in the queue. When the soup contained onions, the place to be was at the front, as the onions floated to the top. When the soup contained rice, it was better at the back, because rice sinks to the bottom. Each room in each sector organised a roster of skilly carriers from the kitchen to the serving point. Every prisoner was also allowed three mugs of tea a day, brewed by the cooks and distributed in similar fashion.

The sheer monotony of the official routine pervaded all aspects of everyday existence. In between the roll calls and feeding times, those men who were fit enough indulged in endless walks around the compound and the recreational field. During the winter months the view of snow-capped mountains in the distance provided a welcome distraction. Other staple pastimes were hanging around chatting in groups and simply dozing on the bunks.

By now the supply of Red Cross parcels for the POWs was more regular, a factor which improved the overall health level of prisoners and in many cases probably saved their lives. At its best level, each man received a parcel on a weekly basis. Red Cross parcels gave prisoners a better balanced diet. Wally certainly grew stronger during this period. Two kinds of Red Cross parcel were received – British and Canadian. A typical British parcel contained tins of stew, meatloaf, sardines, cheese, creamed rice and condensed milk, plus tea, sugar, a bar of chocolate and 10 cigarettes. The Italians made a point of stabbing all the tins, so that they could not be stored for use in an escape attempt. Red Cross parcel days always triggered auctions of contents in the field, as well as the exchange of items between prisoners such as food for cigarettes. Furthermore, soap from the parcels was often bartered for bread with the Italian guards.

A lack of warm clothing in the winter months was a serious problem for the POWs, many of whom were captured in shirts and shorts in the heat of North Africa. The men were grateful to have their two blankets issued upon arrival at PG53 (along with a bowl and a spoon). At the end of February 1943 a large consignment of warm clothing arrived at the camp, which eased the discomfort. Also the first consignment of next of kin parcels appeared in January, most of which included clothing and food, including large bars of chocolate. Another of Wally's stories concerned one man who devoured a large bar of chocolate in one go. He died in hospital the next day, having burst the lining of his stomach, unused as his body was to such a volume of food. This story is confirmed in one of the accounts written by inmates of PG53.

Severe overcrowding in the bunk rooms meant that ventilation became a problem. The pervading smell was of unwashed bodies and night latrines. Some prisoners did not bother to wash, and water was not always available for the more hygienic. There was a distinct improvement in April 1943 with the introduction of new showers. For many it was the first hot shower for a long time, although each POW was limited to 2-3 minutes, owing to the scarcity of fuel. The men found it difficult to sleep in winter, due to a combination of the bitter cold and their fellow bunk inhabitants, bedbugs and lice. It was a common sight on sunny days to see prisoners sat outside trying to delouse themselves. The Swiss Red Cross reported that 52 POWs died at camp PG53 between November 1942 and May 1943, 39 of them from pneumonia. At least the three-monthly visits by the Swiss Red Cross resulted in the prisoners receiving better treatment from the Italians.

According to the Geneva Convention, POWs were entitled to send two letters and four postcards a month. All mail was censored, so little information of note can be gleaned from items sent home. Only one of Wally's letters has survived, written to his mother on 2nd January 1943. It tells of having Christmas pudding and Christmas cake on Christmas day. A section of the letter had been blacked out by the censor.

PG53 developed an active social life in order to better pass the time. As well as the organised football and cricket matches according to season, more sedentary games such as chess and 'housey-housey' (bingo) were played regularly. Given his knee injury sustained whilst playing football in India, Wally favoured a game of chess or draughts. A band was formed in each sector, with sector 3 even having someone who had played with the renowned Ambrose orchestra pre-war. At Christmas 1942 the men staged a pantomime entitled 'Ali Baba and his Four Cronies', a good laugh was enjoyed by all. In March 1943 prisoners staged an arts and crafts display. One of the most imaginative creations at PG53 was a large working clock made from Klim milk tins (found in Canadian Red Cross parcels) by a pre-war watchmaker named Len Burch. The camp commandant came to see it and was most impressed.

Another venture set up by inmates of the camp was a daily newspaper. Every morning at 8am the latest news snippets and rumours of the day were posted on a notice board outside one of the buildings. A large crowd would gather to read the latest developments, particularly with reference to the progress of the war. In this way the POWs were able to counter the Italian propaganda bulletins, which told a very different tale. Loudspeakers were set up in the camp by the Italians, and propaganda was broadcast at least once a fortnight.

The men's morale was boosted by learning of Allied victories/advances. For instance, on 25th January 1943 the fall of Tripoli, 9th May the capture of Tunis, 9th June the surrender of Pantelleria, and most significantly the invasion of Sicily on 9th July, which coincided with the staging of an inter-sector sports day. The invasion of Sicily led to the first discussions among POWs of breaking out of the camp to rejoin the British troops, once they had reached the Italian mainland. Also this event panicked the Italian captors into herding all the men into their bunk rooms, and additional machine guns were mounted and aimed in the direction of the accommodation blocks.

March 1943 witnessed the arrival of the warm days of spring, which provided another boost to the mood of the prisoners. They were able to sit out all day in the sun, smoking cigarettes and playing cards. The will to survive was a crucial component in an individual's morale. Wally certainly possessed this to a high degree. Comradeship was also a powerful binding force, and Wally did have comrades from the Kings Own regiment in the camp. Army regulars tended to look down on conscripts and territorials in the camp. Wally expressed this view on many occasions.

On 25th July 1943, Mussolini was overthrown and a new Italian government formed under Marshall Badoglio. It was now clear that Italian enthusiasm for participating in the war was waning (except among committed Fascist supporters). In August the weather was hot and oppressive, and the men stayed outside until the early hours. Also in this month there were regular concerts, provided by one of the two dance orchestras or the military band. Up to 2,000 prisoners were allowed to attend a concert. On 4th September 1943, Allied troops landed in Calabria on the Italian mainland. Plans were now discussed in earnest by the POWs regarding possible release or escape from the camp. Preparations were made for escape such as the bartering of Red Cross clothing for packets of biscuits from the Italian guards. According to the visiting Swiss Red Cross at the beginning of September, PG53 contained 7,437 prisoners, all but 22 of which were British.

9. <u>The armistice on 8th September 1943</u>

On the evening of September 8th the Italian driver of a ration truck began shouting *armistizio* and hugging everyone within range. The Italians had agreed an armistice with the Allies. An excited crowd gathered as the news spread like lightning through the camp. Shortly afterwards the *commandante* informed the camp over the loudspeaker, that he had not yet received anything official and prisoners should stay calm. Almost simultaneously, bonfires were lit on the hillsides all around, where noisy celebrations of peace were heard late into the night. The official announcement on Italian radio had taken place at 7.22pm.

The events which took place over the next week, leading up to the mass escape on the 15th, are clearly documented. However, the exact chronology varies in different accounts. For instance, the handover of control of the camp to the British is variously given as the 9th, 10th or 11th. An incident involving the cutting of the wire is described as being on the 9th, 11th or 13th. Exactly what happened on the 15th, and in what order, is also subject to different versions. From the two detailed book length accounts by inmates and the 126 escape reports consulted, I have deduced the most likely sequence of events.

In the morning (9th September) a thanksgiving service was held in the field, at the conclusion of which the men gave a hearty rendition of 'God Save the King'. Endless discussions reverberated among the POWs as to whether to try and escape, or wait in the camp for the Allied forces to arrive. Wally and his comrades in the Kings Own decided to escape at the first available opportunity. A complication existed in the form of the stay put order issued by Military Intelligence to the Senior British Officers in POW camps in Italy. Military Intelligence feared the possibility of mass reprisals, if the 42,000 British prisoners in Italy were to break out. Instead they suggested a policy of individual escapees, in order to bring relevant information to the advancing Allies.

A tense atmosphere reigned as the Italian guards were still in place. Finally on September 11th the *commandante* received instructions to withdraw the armed guards from inside the camp, but retain sentries on the wire and at the gates. Internal command of the camp was handed to the Senior British Officer (SBO), Captain Frewin, who was a medical officer. At 7pm in an evening broadcast to the POWs, the SBO requested that they remain patient and await further developments. The orders remained not to escape, but to stay in camp.

The next day (12th) was a quiet day, disrupted only by a German plane, which circled the camp a couple of times. After the armistice German reinforcements were sent into Italy from the north, and they began to look for Allied POW camps. Their plan was to take over the camps and send the prisoners to camps in Germany. On the other hand, camp commandants were under instructions from the Italian War Office to prevent British POWs falling into German hands.

On the evening of the 13th, some of the prisoners decided to attempt an escape. A crowd gathered on the outer perimeter of the recreational field and the wire was cut, as Italian guards looked on, uncertain as to what to do. However, the *commandante* Colonel Petragnani was informed, and he came running up and fired over the heads of the POWs, who backed off. All prisoners were herded away from the field and back to the compound. The *commandante* informed the SBO that he would have one hour's notice of any approaching Germans, and at this point the camp gates would be opened. The SBO reaffirmed that the men were to stay put, and anyone escaping without permission would be subject to a court martial. Behind the scenes, senior NCOs countermanded this, on the grounds that it was a British soldier's duty to try to escape and disrupt the enemy.

An increasing number of Italian guards began to leave their posts and desert. Most of them were conscripts who wanted to go home now that the war (from the Italian viewpoint) was over. Their philosophy was '*tutti a casa*'. A new consignment of Red Cross parcels had arrived in early September, and all of these were distributed to the men in readiness for a possible departure from the camp. Everyone stocked up with food and other items such as soap and cigarettes, which could be bartered for bread.

10. Mass escape on 15th September

By the 15th there were barely a dozen guards left outside the camp. Captain Frewin left by car to visit PG70 at Monte Urano (around 35 km away) to discuss the situation with the SBO there. He didn't get there, as there was already a German presence in the area. Whilst Frewin was away, even more Italian guards abandoned their posts. Suddenly the inmates were in total control of the camp. An orgy of looting and destruction ensued as a crowd invaded the Italian officers quarters and the Italian canteen. Months of repression were unleashed on enemy property.

More significantly, someone commandeered a spade and smashed the lock on the main gate, and the side gates were also opened. The last remaining Italian guards fled in panic. Acting SBO, RSM Burgess, told the POWs to pack their kit and stand by. Many took this as a cue to leave through the now open gates. Shortly after, Captain Frewin returned and ordered the prisoners to stay put. He requested volunteers to guard the camp. This resulted in another wave of men opting for freedom outside the camp, before the volunteers could be mustered.

A fascinating picture of the mass escape can be gleaned from the 126 escape reports and the two detailed accounts. The timing of the opening of the gates is variously given as 3pm, 3.30pm and 4pm. Estimates as to the number of prisoners who escaped ranges from 800 to 3,000. A variety of exits were employed, most common was walking out of the main gate, whilst others left by the side gates, the gap in the wire, and in one case, over the wall.

Those POWs who remained behind in the camp were soon in captivity again. At 1am on the 16th, around 300 German troops and several armoured vehicles arrived at PG53 to take control of the camp. The Germans had come from PG70, which had been retaken a few hours earlier (hence explaining Frewin's failure to get there). Later that day a German roll call established that 1,800 prisoners had escaped from PG53. Within days those POWs who stayed in camp were shipped to Germany by train. One of the accounts suggests that, in typical British fashion, around 400 men walked out of the camp on the 15th and simply went into the village and got drunk. Doubtless many of these were recaptured.

11. Escape with four others and head south

According to Wally's escape report in the War Office archives (there are in fact two reports, in WO 208/3319 and WO 208/5395), the camp gates were opened at about 3pm on the 15th. The guards had deserted and anybody could have left. He walked out of the main gate with four others, three of them comrades from the Kings Own (Cpl Norris, Cpl Ratcliffe and Pte Foulkes), and the fourth a private in the Scots Guards. It is likely that Wally's group was among the first wave of escapees, shortly after the gates were opened, as they had prepared to leave at the first possible opportunity. Their plan was to head south in the direction of the British lines. The 8th Army had landed at Taranto and was known to be advancing up the Adriatic coast.

My account of Wally's escape route is based on a variety of sources. First, his escape report outlines the main points along the route, culminating in reaching the British lines at Guglionesi on 15th October. Second, Wally's regularly repeated stories confirmed other places and events along the way. Third, three of Wally's photos from the army in India, which he retained throughout the war, have a string of Italian village names written on the back. Fourth, written accounts by other escapees provide useful additional information. Finally, my own journey in September and October 2009, which attempted to trace and follow his route, filled in many of the missing pieces. When in the field trying to work out how to get from A to B, the solution often appears self-evident. As a result of combining all these sources, I am confident of around 90% of the route.

Wally's group of five went out of the main gate and turned right along the main road south towards Ascoli. After passing the end of the camp wall, they passed the hydroelectric station on the right and crossed the first of many bridges. The bridge over the Chienti river is viewed (symbolically) through a wire fence in figure 7.

figure 7 the first bridge over the Chienti river

Initially the main aim was to put some distance between themselves and the camp. After crossing the bridge a ridge of low hills was directly ahead. The road veered to the right before the climb up the hill to the ridge, which the unfit men found hard work.

At the top of the hill they looked back to check if they were being followed, but all they saw were other groups of escaping POWs heading along the road. Figure 8 looks back from the ridge. The road winds up from the bridge, the camp is beyond the trees on the left, and the town of Macerata is visible on the hill.

figure 8 looking back from the first hill

Continuing along the main road the group encountered a vineyard on the right, followed quickly by an orchard. They were witnessing first hand that the Marche is the garden of Italy, meaning that there was an abundance of local produce. Around four km into the walk on the edge of a wood, a large building emerged on the left. They were wary in case it was a military institution and proceeded under the cover of trees on the far side of the road. However, the large Romanesque-Gothic structure turned out to be the *Abbadia di Fiastra*, a Cistercian abbey.

A couple of kilometres further down the road, the men reached the hamlet of Maesta. It consisted of a few detached stone farmhouses set back from the road. From one of these a family of peasants came running out carrying baskets, from which they produced bread, cheese and fruit to give to the escapers. A jug of wine was also furnished. This was the group's first refreshment stop. Quite possibly it was the farmhouse pictured in figure 9.

Set back from the road, the original stone farmhouse is white with a roof covered in red tiles. The brick outbuildings are a more recent addition. This farmhouse is typical of the area. The ground floor was occupied by the animals, mainly cows, hence the small windows. The upper floor with larger windows was for the peasant family.

figure 9 traditional stone farmhouse in Maesta

After over a year spent as a prisoner in various Italian camps, Wally was extremely hostile to the Italians. He described his attitude at the time as "I would as soon shoot an Italian as look at him". Most of the men were distrustful and contemptuous of the Italians. Hence Wally's group were genuinely surprised at the warmth of their reception from the peasant family. Having experienced only the Fascist officers and conscripted guards, they were unprepared for the friendliness and generosity of the *contadini*.

A couple of kilometres further down the road, the group reached the village of Convento, an elongated settlement with a cluster of houses on either side of the road. At the entrance to the village, a detached farmhouse again offered refreshment, as well as the possibility of sleeping accommodation in the outhouse. It was a warm evening, and now more relaxed in the company of the *contadini*, the men enjoyed sitting and sipping wine.

The farmhouse is again set back from the main road, hence away from the prying eyes of any vehicles on the main road. It has the same layout of humans upstairs and animals downstairs, and the outhouse is on the left, connecting to the animal quarters.

figure 10 farmhouse in Convento – the first night?

Convento is overlooked by the hilltop town of Urbisaglia, which dates back to Roman times. Vineyards and orchards are dotted on the slopes below. The escapees were warned to avoid Urbisaglia, as it was known as a centre of Fascist support. Indeed in general it was in the towns that Fascist support was concentrated.

figure 11 the hilltop town of Urbisaglia

The following morning the escapees were advised to get off the main road by the family. Wally never forgot this Italian phrase "*prende la piccolo strada*". This was sensible advice although the road was not a main artery. Most German transport heading north-south used the broader coastal road. However within days, German trucks were a common sight on the Ascoli road.

Accordingly the group turned left off the main road just past Convento, and took a small road winding up for 5 km towards Loro Piceno. An invigorating sense of freedom engulfed the five men, as they wandered past fields and gazed at the hills. Many of the fields displayed circular stacks of hay, built round a central pole with a conical top. Off to the right, the daunting mass of the Sibillini mountains edged into view. After passing through a large wood, the road took a sharp bend and climbed up to the hilltop settlement of Loro Piceno.

The last part of the climb into Loro Piceno was steep, which left some of the men out of breath. It seemed to take forever to reach there, when the church spire had been visible for a long time. They didn't need to enter Loro Piceno, as just on the edge of town there was a right turn for Sant Angelo in Ponatana, their next target.

figure 12 the road winds up to the hilltop settlement of Loro Piceno

Wally's group ploughed on. The road headed sharply downhill, with the Sibillini mountains now straight ahead. Another climb followed to San Lorenzo, from where there were great views in several directions. Down again they went from San Lorenzo, and then a steady rise to L'Immacolata, and on upward to Sant Angelo.

The second night was spent on the outskirts of Sant Angelo at a farmhouse, where the hospitality was again generous. All the men were given a warm heartening bowl of soup, which was a kind of minestrone. It was at Sant Angelo after two days of walking that the group of five came to the decision to split into a two and a three. They judged that five men walking together were too conspicuous, and there had been reports of Germans nearby actively seeking to round up escapees, as well as the ever present threat of Fascist informers. Wally was part of the three along with two Kings Own comrades, and before setting off the next day he consulted a map of the area at the local school. All schools had been closed by the authorities, so access was easily arranged via the local schoolmaster. Throughout his journey Wally often got to see a map or obtained route information with the help of local school teachers or local priests.

17

At this point I am unsure as to the exact detail of the next part of Wally's route. The school map indicated that the next major obstacle was the river Tenna, over which there were two bridges, if one wanted to avoid the crossing on the main road. It is likely that one group headed for one bridge, and the second group aimed for the other. I have chosen to describe the route via Penna San Giovanni and Monte San Martino, which is the most direct line towards Ascoli.

Wally's threesome walked downhill from Sant Angelo, and turned right for Penna San Giovanni. A tiring up and down sequence followed as all the villages were on the hilltops, and regular rest stops were the order of the day. They skirted around Penna as it was quite a large settlement.

figure 13 looking back up to Penna San Giovanni on the ridge

After Penna the men took a turning for Monte San Martino. A long zigzag descent led to the valley bottom, the high mountain range was now visible to the right. Inevitably a long winding climb followed, until they saw the walls of Monte San Martino straight ahead. Another sizeable settlement, the escapees did not enter.

figure 14 the Sibillini mountains viewed from the vicinity of Monte San Marino

Instead the trio took a left turn downhill, passing through fields of corn. After a long day of endless ups and downs the men were exhausted. A small track led off to the right heading for the hamlet of Molino. Thankfully the *contadini* of Molino provided much welcome sustenance and a sleeping place for the night. After supper the men were urged to exchange their uniforms for civilian clothing. Wally swapped with an old man from a neighbouring farm. He would spend the rest of the journey in a peasant's jacket and trousers, along with a kind of black beret. Blending in with the locals would be crucial to evading recapture. Whereas the Italians always knew from the escapees' deportment and mannerisms that they were *inglese*, the Germans couldn't tell the difference.

In the morning the guests were given the standard peasant breakfast of dry bread and bitter acorn coffee. From Molino it was not far downhill to the river Tenna. Crossing the bridge over the river proved straightforward in the end, although Wally approached with a degree of caution. All three men crouched in a ditch and watched the main road, which was heading east-west. It was clear, so Wally was the first to cross the little stone bridge and take cover on the other side of the river. One by one the others followed, and the whole procedure was completed with no traffic in sight.

After the bridge the three men set off on a long climb uphill in the direction of Montefalcone Appennino. They passed through a forested area, eventually emerging even higher than Monte San Martino on the hilltop on the opposite side of the valley. Here the landscape was dotted with orchards, most of them dripping with fruit.

For the first week of the walk, the grape harvest was in full swing. Wally recalled witnessing the age old tradition of treading the grapes with bare feet. On one occasion, one of his comrades had a go at treading, regarding it as part payment for their supper.

figure 15 grapes ready for harvesting near Montefalcone Appennino

On the hillside just below Montefalcone Appennino, the three escapees stopped at a well-to-do farmhouse with large orchards (figure 16 possibly?). They were warmly welcomed by the family, given plentiful food and comfortable accommodation in the barn. An additional attraction was the presence of two beautiful teenage daughters.

figure 16 large farmhouse with orchards below Montefalcone Appennino

Wally's two comrades were very taken with the two girls, and when the father suggested that they were welcome to stay at the farm and await the arrival of the British forces, they were keen to accept the offer. Wally was more cautious and warned of the danger of a local fascist informing the authorities that some men were staying at this farm. In this scenario, not only would the escapees be recaptured, but reprisals were likely against the family and their property. After days of walking up hill and down dale, Wally's comrades were very tired and decided to stay on at the farm. Wally had resolved from the beginning to stay no more than one night at a location, so he resisted the temptation and headed south on his own the next day.

12. Head south alone

Travelling on his own, Wally could proceed slightly faster, in that there were no collective decisions to be arrived at, as he was responsible only for himself. The key decisions every day were which route to take each morning, and then later in the day, which house to stop at. By late afternoon it was necessary to look for shelter for the night, as a curfew came into force at 8pm. He possessed the discipline and decisiveness of a trained soldier, traits most useful in evading recapture. The main obstacles to be overcome were main roads and large rivers, as well as keeping an eye out for German troops on the move or Fascist militia.

Wally's attitude to the Italian people was totally transformed by his experience of the hospitality and bravery of the peasant farmers. Food and wine were freely offered. He quickly learned to say *per favore* (please), *mangia* (eat), *grazie* (thank you) and other simple words. He often told of a set routine of approaching a farmhouse and asking for *acqua* (water), to be routinely told *acqua niente buono* (water not good). Instead he would be offered a glass of wine, which he would consume and then say *buono* (good), and immediately receive a second glass, which was praised as *molto buono* (very good). A filling repast with glasses of wine at lunchtime would occasionally require a siesta, before moving on.

Sleeping accommodation provided was mostly in the barn or in the cowshed. The welcome and generosity of the *contadini* was overwhelming given that most of them were poor. They did not have what would be regarded as standard home comforts in England such as electricity, gas, mains water, carpets etc. A written account by a fellow escapee in Italy outlines the careful choice of which farmhouse to approach. A farmhouse with five haystacks was rich and possibly *Fascisti*, whereas only one haystack indicated that the family was too poor to be able to feed extra mouths. Three haystacks was just right.

Frequently, Wally was accompanied in the morning by the old man in the family, who would lead him to the next small path and point out the trail ahead. Their bravery was evident in that the Germans offered a reward for information leading to the recapture of a POW. Those families who helped escapees could be shot and/or have their farms burned to the ground. The German decree regarding the death penalty for helpers was issued on 19th September, only four days after Wally escaped.

Many of the peasant families had sons who were away with the Italian military, which led them to empathise with the escapers, especially the mothers. Some had sons who had deserted after the armistice and were themselves on the run. Others had sons who had been taken prisoner by the British in North Africa (fully 300,000 by early 1941). Worst of all were those with sons fighting on the Russian front.

Wally set off on his own along the road up to Montefalcone Appennino. He avoided entering the town by turning right just outside the walls, and heading along an avenue of trees. At the end of the avenue the road turned left into a tunnel through the rock beneath the town. Out the other side were almond trees beneath the steep cliffs (see left).

figure 17 looking back up to Montefalcone Appennino

For several of Wally's other tales, the exact location is not known. His first experience of needing to defecate whilst in a farmhouse caused him considerable embarrassment, as the farmhouse didn't have indoor facilities. When he requested the toilet, the family pointed outside, and when outside they pointed to the field. He walked some distance into the field, and still they were all watching him, and indicating that was the place.

Wally also described witnessing the boiling of tomatoes in a large iron pot in order to make tomato puree. Similarly he saw the preparation of polenta, made from maize and resembling a kind of yellow porridge. The ritual of eating polenta was certainly a novel experience. When ready the polenta was poured onto the kitchen table, tomato puree and grated cheese were added on top, and then everyone would dig in, each from a different edge of the table. Occasionally if a family had any meat, usually rabbit or fowl, a few pieces were placed in the centre. He who ate the polenta the fastest, and reached the centre first, would get more of the meat.

Most of the hospitable peasant families were curious about their visitor. They particularly wanted to know *dove venire* (where come from) and *dove andare* (where going). Another regular theme concerned questions about *famiglia* (family). Wally showed them some photos, including those of his sister's young children. He had great difficulty in convincing them that these were not his own children.

Returning to Wally's route, he headed down towards Faveto beneath the cliffs of Montefalcone (figure 17). After passing through Faveto, Wally reached a main provincial road leading to the coast at Pedaso. He needed to turn right and proceed along this road for two kilometres, before turning left onto a minor road. On this stretch of road lay a series of culverts to cope with (mostly dry) streams descending from the steep slopes. It was whilst traversing these culverts that he heard the distant rumble of military vehicles, and hurriedly hid in one of the culverts under the road. This was one of the scariest moments of his month long walk, as a whole German brigade passed overhead. Fortunately, no vehicle stopped in order to answer a call of nature, or for any other reason.

With great relief Wally quickly completed the stretch along the valley road, and turned left over a little bridge across the river Aso. Soon the minor road ascended into woodland, terrain in which he felt more secure. His next target was Force, a small town on the ridge above. He was told to take a right turn at Force for Venarotta, and follow the minor road along the top of the ridge towards Ascoli. The ridge road ran parallel to the main road in the valley below. Along the ridge there were good views to the right and the left, as the roadside alternated between grassland and woodland. On the outskirts of Venarotta, Wally turned right to head down towards the main road from Amandola to Ascoli (SP237). He was advised by an English speaking schoolteacher to avoid the large city of Ascoli. His best bet was to go along the main road from Amandola for 6 kilometres until it met the major Roma-Ascoli road, and cross straight over to reach an area of remote minor roads (*Monti della Laga* or Mountains of the Lakes). All well and good, but walking along the main road for 6 kilometres was risky. Accordingly an old man from the village Wally spent the night in, offered to accompany him along this stretch.

In the morning they walked together, both in peasant outfits and wearing berets, sagely observed and recognised for who they were by local people, but unnoticed by the occasional Germans passing in army vehicles, or taking refreshment at a roadside café. Wally had grown confident enough to mumble '*buon giorno*' to the German soldiers, as the Italians tended to do. He received the same dismissive scowl as the locals did. The Germans couldn't spot the cuckoo in the nest. Crossing the Roma-Ascoli main road was a potential hazard, as it provided a route to the coast for heavy German traffic. Fortunately the road was clear as the two men reached the junction. A short dog's leg was required, over the road, turn left for a few hundred metres, then right onto a minor road towards Taverna di Mezzo. Once safely on the side road, the old man wished Wally good luck and returned to his village.

Wally had been briefed by the school teacher on the journey ahead. He needed to cross a high ridge to the left in order to reach the *Monti della Laga* area. Accordingly, Wally turned left in Taverna and began a long steep winding climb through woodland. About halfway up he passed the tiny village of Funti. From here, birds of prey could be seen hovering above the ridge.

The climb up to the ridge was exhausting, but eventually Wally reached the hamlet of Talvacchia, perched on top of the ridge. Talvacchia stood above a steep cliff, overlooking a deep valley containing the Castellano river. On the other side of the valley, the *Monti di Fiore* (mountains of flowers) were clearly visible.

Wally accepted refreshment from a local family, before being directed down a track to the river valley below. The family had a plentiful supply of logs ready for the harsh winter.

figure 18 trail down to the river from Talvacchia

The trail down from Talvacchia through the wood led in 1943 to a small bridge over the river. This was replaced in 1960 by a dam. The houses in Talvacchia are just visible on the top of the ridge.

figure 19 the modern day dam beneath Talvacchia

Wally had now reached a remote backwater, unlikely to encounter German visitors. He followed the deep forested valley southwards for around 8 km, the SP49 road hugging the left bank of the river. On retracing the route in 2009, I encountered a group of locals gathered around a large bubbling cauldron of polenta. Probably Wally's polenta story happened somewhere around here. Another uphill climb led from the river to Valle Castellana, the largest settlement in the area, though only a village. Beyond here the roads became even narrower, and the population sparser.

Wally followed the road up through Pascellata and Paranesi, before taking a trail down to Caiano. He continued along the narrow roads in a generally southerly direction. Now for the first time the Gran Sasso mountain range loomed ahead, a formidable barrier Wally would have to negotiate.

figure 20 the first hazy view of the Gran Sasso looming ahead

Farmhouses were few and far between in this section. Wally was as likely to encounter goats on the road, as I did in 2009.

figure 21 goats on the road

The next target was Cortino, a village reached on a minor winding road, passing through open grassland with fewer trees and more sheep. It is hunting country at this time of year. In 2009 I witnessed a large group of hunters near Servillo. It is likely that Wally also came across hunters in this area.

13. The Gran Sasso

From Cortino, the road headed down towards Crognaleto. Somewhere in this area Wally made contact with a group of partisans, who offered to escort him over the next major obstacle, the Gran Sasso. This mountain range is the highest in the Appenines, rising to over 2,600 metres. There are trails which traverse high passes in the range, but detailed local knowledge is required to avert getting lost on the mountain.

Wally set off from Crognaleto accompanied by two partisans, who were to be his fellow travellers for the next few days. They proceeded through a deep valley, with the dark brooding mass of the Gran Sasso towering straight ahead at the bottom of the valley. A secondary hazard, to be negotiated prior to the Gran Sasso, was crossing the major road from Roma towards Teramo, which was subject to a lot of German transport. Immediately before the major road was a bridge over the Vomano river. A small group of German soldiers was stationed at the far end of the bridge, where it adjoins the main road.

Initially, Wally and the partisans observed the bridge from behind a clump of trees. Eventually, after a prolonged period of observation, they judged it reasonably safe to proceed as the soldiers were not stopping or hindering pedestrians from crossing the bridge.

figure 22 view of Aprati bridge from behind the trees

The trio walked casually past the Germans, not forgetting to wish them *buon giorno*. Wally was growing more confident of his ability to pass muster as an Italian, with the Germans at least, but never with The Italians.

figure 23 looking straight across Aprati bridge

At the junction with the main road, they turned right and strolled through Aprati, an elongated village at the base of the cliff. They followed the road along the dark gloomy gorge for about a kilometre, and then turned sharp left up a minor road to the village of Nerito, passing through a densely wooded area.

Nerito is the starting point for a trail up to and over the Gran Sasso. The early part of the trail through woodland was a hive of activity, with local women picking *porcini* mushrooms, and donkeys carrying loads of wood.

figure 24 the Nerito trail leading up to the Gran Sasso

On this early part of the trail, Wally probably passed by local charcoal burners, as I did in 2009. They store piles of timber in a pinnacle or pyramid shape, and were much more numerous in 1943.

figure 25 a wood stack along the Nerito trail

The trek with the partisans up the Nerito trail and over the pass through the Gran Sasso was the most arduous part of Wally's escape route. However, it was rendered manageable by the fact that he was not alone. In addition to companionship, the partisans brought knowledge of the location of refuges along the mountain trail, which were wooden huts in which to break journey overnight.

The trail from the Gran Sasso comes down near the village of San Pietro. In total they had walked around 20 km from the village of Nerito, much of it over difficult terrain.

figure 26 the trail down from the Gran Sasso near San Pietro

Looking back, Wally could see the barren hills of the Gran Sasso, which they had just traversed. The trail they took came through the pass visible in the photo.

figure 27 view of the pass through the Gran Sasso

After such a long trek through the mountains, the trio almost certainly took shelter and refreshment in the village of San Pietro. It is perched on a hilltop with a steep drop on one side.

figure 28 looking down on San Pietro village

From San Pietro there was a steep winding descent into the tourist resort of Fonte Cerreto. There was, and is, accommodation for walkers in summer and skiers in winter. A funicular takes skiers up to the ski resort at the top.

figure 29 looking down towards Fonte Cerreto

On reaching Fonte Cerreto, the trio passed La Villetta, a small inn. The two partisans proudly pointed it out to Wally, and informed him that their partisan unit had held Benito Mussolini (the former Italian dictator) prisoner there for a couple of days, about one month before.

figure 30 La Villetta where Mussolini was held in August 1943

Around 26th August 1943 Mussolini was brought to Fonte Cerreto by his partisan captors. He stayed at La Villetta for two nights, before being transferred to the supposedly safer location of the ski hotel at the top of the funicular. He was rescued by German papatroopers led by Lieutenant-Colonel Otto Skorzeny on 12th September, only 3 days before Wally escaped from PG53.

From Fonte Cerreto, the trio took the road to Castel del Monte, which winds gradually up through a wooded area. Visible off to the left was the main spine of the Gran Sasso. Wally was relieved that he had not had to cross these higher peaks.

figure 31the main spine of the Gran Sasso mountain range

After awhile the scenery changed to rolling grassland. This was excellent terrain for walking, and they set off on a trail across the grassland towards Castel del Monte.

figure 32 the rolling grassland of the Gran Sasso

In 1943 the weather was fine in late September, as it was in 2009, with clear blue skies and warm sunshine. The autumn trees were particularly beautiful.

figure 33 autumn trees on the Gran Sasso

Wally and his two companions will most certainly have met with a shepherd and his sheep, as I did in 2009. This traditional scene has remained unchanged for centuries.

figure 34 a shepherd and his sheep on the Gran Sasso

After around 20 km of gentle walking on the rolling grassland, the trail descends into Castel del Monte, a fortified settlement which occupies a stunning hilltop location. The town itself is full of narrow streets, narrower alleys, and steep interconnecting steps. The dominant church can be seen for miles around.

figure 35 looking down on Castel del Monte

Wally and his two comrades stayed the night with a family of partisans in Castel del Monte. Next morning, having completed their task, his two companions of the last few days wished him well, said goodbye and headed back across the Gran Sasso. From Castel del Monte, the partisans pointed in the distance to the unmistakable mass of the Maiella, another mountain range Wally would have to cross to reach the British front line on the other side. Having just completed the exacting transit of the Gran Sasso, his reaction was "Another Bloody Mountain", which serves well as a description of the whole escape route.

Wally set off again on his own, and the next target was the Forca di Penne pass. A long winding descent led into an area full of orchards around Villa Santa Lucia. Just before the pass, the road hangs on the edge of a steep drop to the right, into a wide U-shaped valley. After the pass, he took a right turn for Corvara, and there was now a steep drop on the left hand side, down to the plain below. He passed through Colli, a village on the top of the ridge.

The village of Corvara sits on a bare rock ridge, and gives the impression of hanging from the rock. After Corvara, Wally headed down a winding road through woods, orchards and olive groves towards the Pescara river valley.

figure 36 the village of Corvara hanging from the rock

Crossing the Pescara valley was one of the most dangerous sections of the entire route, as the valley was a major corridor for German activity. Several written accounts by escapees talk of turning back at this point, unable to find a safe place to cross. An escapee had to negotiate not only the Pescara river, but also the Roma-Pescara major road, and the Roma-Pescara main railway line. The partisans informed Wally that all the bridges were guarded by German troops. However, they knew of a weak link in the chain.

Accordingly, Wally took a trail down to the *Diga di Alanno* (Alanno dam). Here was a hydroelectric station with a walkway along the top of the dam. The power station is now disused, but the walkway is still visible.

figure 37 the hydroelectric station and road leading to the walkway

Access to the hydroelectric station was via a small road, leading off from the Roma-Pescara road, and going under two tunnels, beneath road and rail. Hence it was possible to cross the river, the railway and the road, all within a few hundred metres at this point. Although the area was swarming with power station workers during the day, at night it was patrolled only by a night watchman. As of yet there were no Germans guarding this route. Wally waited until dark and then approached the dam with caution. In the end he was able to cross the dam, and pass under the two tunnels quickly, without any problems. In figure 38 the nearest tunnel is under the railway, and the furthest under the road.

figure 38 the two tunnels under the railway and the road

The road under the two tunnels led directly to a track up the hillside towards the Caramanico road. The track passes through vineyards and cultivated fields.

figure 39 the trail winding up from the two tunnels

14. The Maiella

The minor S487 road heads to Caramanico and then Campo di Giove, and Wally was to follow this for over 50 kilometres. Initially it climbs up from the Pescara valley to San Valentino in Abruzzi, his next target of Caramanico was 22 kilometres along the road. This area was extensively wooded, which provided plenty of cover when a very occasional suspect vehicle came along the road. As Wally reached the plateau, two massive mountain ridges began to dominate the landscape. To the right was *Monte Marrone* (chestnut mountain), and to the left the Maiella. The formidable barrier of the Maiella, which rises to over 2,700 metres, would have to be surmounted at some point in order to reach the British front line on the other side.

Eventually Caramanico came into view, nestled on a steep wooded hillside, beneath a rocky promontory, and with the main spine of the Maiella visible behind.

figure 40 looking ahead to Caramanico

According to several written accounts, many British POWs were hiding out in the Caramanico area, after escaping from a prison camp nearby. It is likely that Wally encountered some of these men, but nonetheless he maintained his resolve to keep going. In Caramanico he was advised as to the best way to get over the Maiella.

Leaving Caramanico, Wally continued along the road towards the San Leonardo pass. The imposing main spine of the Maiella drew ever nearer on the left. By the roadside, the terrain alternated between grassland and woodland.

figure 41 main spine of the Maiella

After passing through Sant Eufemia, and bypassing Roccacaramanico on a hilltop to the right, Wally reached the *Passo San Leonardo*. From here he looked back and saw the Gran Sasso in the distance. He had come so far, but still had some way to go. Indeed, yet another bloody mountain.

figure 42 looking back to the Gran Sasso in the distance

Beyond the pass, occasional groups of sheep or cows were to be found grazing on the grassland. In 2009 I also saw large wild dogs walking along the road, which looked very much like wolves. Wally may also have seen these rather fearsome creatures. As the road began its descent into Campo di Giove through a wood, Wally spotted a sign pointing to *Fonte Romana* (Roman fountain). He took a pleasant rest stop by the fountain.

On the final approach to Campo di Giove, Wally was relieved to see the promised pass through the Maiella. The trail leading up to the pass was also plainly visible.

figure 43 trail heading up to the pass through the Maiella

Wally skirted around Campo di Giove, as it was a popular tourist resort for skiing in winter and walking in summer. Just past the town, he could see the railway viaduct used to bring in the tourists.

figure 44 the railway viaduct at Campo di Giove

From Campo di Giove, Wally took the trail up and over the Maiella to Palena. The climb was steep and exhausting, but the trail was well-defined through the wood. At the top of the pass, Wally could look ahead to yet another range of hills to be crossed. They were hills rather than mountains, but to Wally, it was just another bloody mountain.

The descent from the pass into Palena is initially through woodland, and then over grassland.

figure 45 trail heading down from the pass to Palena

After partaking of overnight hospitality on the outskirts of Palena, Wally set off on a path across open scrubland to the village of Colledimacine. In the warm sunshine, the village's mainly white houses shone brightly. The solid mass of the Maiella is evident behind.

figure 46 looking ahead to Colledimacine

The next track onward from Colledimacine to Torricella Peligna comes down from the white houses in the centre of the picture. Still the Maiella continues to cast its shadow in the background.

figure 47 the trail down from Colledimacine

On the way to Torricella, Wally passed through fields and woods. There were a few isolated farms, but most of the population round here lived in the hilltop villages.

figure 48 trail heading up to Torricella Peligna

The track is clearly visible in the foreground and to the right. From Torricella, Wally followed the road which heads down to the Sangro river, with the village of Roccascalegna on the hill to the left.

figure 49 Torricella Peligna on the hilltop

Wally's next target was the small town of Bomba, which lay beneath the next ridge of hills. Clearly visible to the left is the pass Wally would take to traverse the hills. First he had to negotiate the bridge over the Sangro river.

figure 50 looking across the valley to Bomba

He proceeded cautiously down the hill towards the bridge. From a distance and behind cover, Wally could see that there were two German sentries on the bridge. Accordingly he waited and observed for some time.

Having seen a couple of Italian peasant farmers walk over the bridge without being hassled, Wally felt confident enough to cross, employing his by now well practised peasant shuffle and a mumbled *buon giorno* to the sentries. After the bridge, he passed Bomba railway station and went uphill through olive groves to the town.

figure 51 the bridge at Bomba

15. The Last Leg

Upon leaving Bomba, Wally was setting off on the last leg of journey. Once up the steep hillside and over the narrow ridge, there would be no more mountain ranges or hill chains to cross. What lay ahead was a landscape dotted with small towns on isolated hillocks, and beyond that the coastal strip, along which the British advance had progressed furthest.

Wally certainly made contact with the resistance movement in Bomba. A surviving photo from Wally's army service in India has Italian names written on the back in pencil, which were probably added in Bomba. The names are written in an old man's hand.

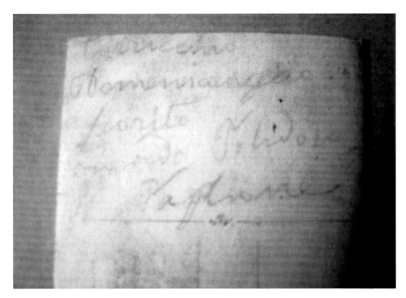

The instructions are to go to the village of Torricchio, which is the other side of the ridge from Bomba, and seek out Domenicangelo Fiorito or Armando (?) Tolidoso. Pagliane may refer to another surname.

figure 52 instructions on the back of a photo

Wally took the trail from Bomba up through the wood and over the ridge. On the other side is a wooded descent into Tornareccio. He went straight through Tornareccio, continuing due east for the three kilometres to Torricchio.

figure 53 trail from Bomba to Tornareccio

The road to Torricchio was lined with farms and orchards. Most probably Wally did make contact with Domenicangelo Fiorito, the first name written on the back of the photo, and stayed overnight in the village.

figure 54 the village of Torricchio

In 2009 the most common surname in the village was Fioriti (possibly the old man's spelling in 1943 was inaccurate), but unfortunately there were no survivors from the Second World War period. Amazingly, two old women in their 80s, Maria and Eliadoro Fioriti respectively, had died within the previous fortnight. Their funeral notices were displayed on the village notice-board. Quite possibly I came that close to discovering someone who had met my father.

In 2009 I encountered a middle aged man named Fioriti, who was making wine in his barn the traditional way. The whole place was swarming with wasps, which was very disconcerting. "Just keep still" he said, but that's not easy to do. Wally may well also have witnessed this process in 1943.

From Torricchio onwards, Wally occasionally saw flashes of light and heard the sounds of battle, emanating from the frontline, some 35-40 kilometres distant. Somebody in Torricchio gave Wally further instructions for the next stage of his journey. Written on the back of a second photo from India are the names of two hilltop towns, roughly due east from Torricchio, Casalanguida and Gissi. Also listed is the Trigno river, which was the last river he would have to cross.

Wally took the track to Casalanguida, passing an area devoted to beekeeping. The perfect sunny weather in 1943 turned around this time, becoming cooler with periods of rain. Now that he was getting so close to the British lines, a spot of bad weather was not going to stop him.

Casalanguida was a town famed for its large market along the main street. From Casalanguida a track runs down through the fields, and then climbs up to the next hill town of Gissi.

figure 55 looking back to Casalanguida

Wally followed a steep ascent through a wood into Gissi. From here he went along the ridge for several kilometres towards the village of San Buono. Onward from San Buono there was a steep descent southward into the Trigno valley, and the last river to be negotiated.

figure 56 the hilltop town of Gissi

After an overnight stop near the village of Tufillo, Wally looked across to Montemitro on the hilltop on the other side of the river. An old narrow stone bridge crossed over the Trigno, which has since been superseded by a larger modern bridge.

figure 57 looking across to Montemitro

Luckily there were no guards on the little bridge, probably because the German forces were concentrated on the next river to the south, the Biferno, which was effectively the frontline at this time. After crossing the bridge, a long winding road climbed steeply up to Montemitro.

In Montemitro, Wally received his final set of directions. A third photo has the name of three towns written on the back, this time in Wally's own hand. Tellingly, two of the names were misspelled, written as they would sound to an Englishman. Hence Palata (*Palata*), Montycilone *(Montecilfone)* and Guloneasi (*Guglionesi*). The three towns form a line in a roughly easterly direction from Montemitro. Beyond them on the coast lies Termoli, which the British had taken in early October.

Wally descended the trail down from the hill town of Montemitro to the plain below. This led on to a track through the woods up to Palata, a distance of around 15 kilometres in total.

figure 58 looking ahead to Palata

Somewhere around Palata, Wally met with an escaped Yugoslav officer, who was too scared to approach the frontline alone. His request to accompany Wally was met with agreement, subject to obeying instructions and keeping silent. German troops were now a regular presence, moving up and down the main road, as well as manning road blocks and defensive positions. The twosome advanced together, probably as far as Montecilfone. By this time Wally was exasperated with his companion, who was generally too noisy, even when in the vicinity of the enemy.

The landscape became more agricultural, as the duo followed a track for 7 kilometres through fields and orchards to the next hill town of Montecilfone. By now the sights and sounds of battle intensified. Early next morning, Wally left the troublesome Yugoslav behind.

figure 59 looking ahead to Montecilfone

Wally skirted around Montecilfone and made for what was to be the last target on his route, the hilltop town of Guglionesi. He followed close to the line of the road, so that he could observe any troop movements.

figure 60 looking ahead to Guglionesi

Several German vehicles headed back in the direction of Montecilfone. There were plenty of olive groves, ditches and hedges for Wally to hide behind. In these early weeks following the Italian armistice, the frontline was relatively fluid and there were gaps between German defensive positions, which he was able to take advantage of.

Approaching one's own frontline is a hazardous undertaking. Wally proceeded with the utmost caution. Suddenly, whilst crouching in a ditch behind a tree, he saw the familiar outline of a British steel helmet.

figure 61meet British patrol just before Guglionesi

"Don't shoot, I'm British", he shouted, and was rapidly surrounded by the reconnaissance patrol. Two of the men were delegated to accompany the scruffy looking 'Italian peasant' back to Guglionesi. For Wally the relief was overwhelming. All his efforts over the past month had been worthwhile.

In 2009, visitors are welcomed to Guglionesi by a sign in four languages, including German. In 1943 the welcome was not so effusive. However, Wally was taken for a blissful beer in a bar in the main square. Afterwards he gave information on German defences to a British officer. Later, he was taken to Termoli, where he was interrogated by a British Intelligence officer.

figure 62 welcome to Guglionesi in four languages

Wally had walked around 438 kilometres (274 miles) in 30 days, much of it through the mountainous central spine of Italy. It had been a superhuman effort. He was one of the earliest to cross the lines heading south in Italy. In the 126 escape reports from PG53 in the War Office archives, only four men reached the British lines before Wally did on 15th October 1943. By the end of November 1943, 988 POWs had crossed the lines without official help i.e. under their own steam.

The days immediately after the armistice afforded the best chance for POWs to get away, before the Germans and Italian fascists regained control. It was also some time before the Germans were able to establish a stable front line, not until the winter of 1943. Interestingly, all three of the men from the Kings Own regiment, whom Wally had initially escaped with, were recaptured, taken to prison camps in Germany, and only repatriated in 1945 at the end of the war. Wally's strategy, of staying only one night at a place, of keeping on the move, and of heading for the next bloody mountain, proved to be the correct choice.

BIBLIOGRAPHY

Absalom, Roger. (1991) *A Strange Alliance: Aspects of Escape and Survival in Italy 1943-45*, Leo S. Olschki Editore, Firenze.

Bains, Lawrence. (1944) *Nine Months Behind the German Lines in Occupied Italy 1943-44*, unpublished manuscript.

Broadbent, Gilbert. (1985) *Behind Enemy Lines*, Anchor Publications, Bognor Regis.

Bullard, Paul. (1989) *Time Off in the Marche*, unpublished manuscript.

Cowper, J. M. (1957) *The Kings Own: The Story of a Royal Regiment Volume III 1914-1950*, Gale and Padden Ltd, Aldershot.

De Souza, Ken. (1989) *Escape from Ascoli*, Newton Publishers, Cowden, Kent.

English, Ian. (ed.) (1997) *Home by Christmas?*, Langlands Edition, Loughborough.

English, Ian. (2004) *Assisted Passage: Walking to Freedom Italy 1943*, Naval and Military Press, Uckfield, East Sussex.

Gilbert, Adrian. (2006) *POW: Allied Prisoners in Europe 1939-1945*, John Murray, London.

Green, Howard. (1972) *The Kings Own Royal Regiment*, Lee Cooper Ltd, London.

Harris, G. H. (1947) *Prisoner of War and Fugitive*, Gale and Padden Ltd, Aldershot.

Lamb, Richard. (1993) *War in Italy 1943-1945: A Brutal Story*, John Murray, London.

Lincolnshire Times, 18 December 1943, 'Escaped P.O.W. Home'.

Millar, J. H. D. (2008) *The Memoirs of J H D Millar*, Quaderni Della Memoria, Servigliano.

Millozzi, Giuseppe. (2007) *Prigonieri Alleati: Cattura, Detenzione E Fuga Nelle Marche 1941-44*, Uguccione Ranieri di Sorbello Foundation, Perugia.

Stockdale, Tom. (1996) *The Life and Times of Benito Mussolini*, Parragon Book Services, Bristol.

Tudor, Malcolm. (2000) *British Prisoners of War in Italy*, Emilia Publishing, Newtown.

Tudor, Malcolm. (2003) *Escape from Italy 1943-45*, Emilia Publishing, Newtown.

War Office Archives, WO208 in the National Archives, 108 escape reports of POWs who travelled south from PG53, and a further 18 escape reports from PG53 in general Escape and Evasion reports: Most importantly, the two escape reports of Wallace Douglas Duke in WO208/5395 and WO208/3319.